The Journey We Shared
Positive Pathways for Teen Parents

Lisa Colla

Cover image © Shutterstock.com

www.innovativeinkpublishing.com
Send all inquiries to:
4050 Westmark Drive
Dubuque, IA 52004-1840

Published in the United States of America

Dedication

To my family, my reason.

Contents

Acknowledgments

First and foremost, I want to thank God for your never ending love and guidance in all I do.

To my husband Jeff Colla, who is also my best friend and rock. You have always encouraged me and let me fly, even when sometimes the landing was not the greatest. You have cheered me on and have always stood by my side. Thank you for letting me chase my dreams and for being the best husband you could ever ask for. I love you more than any words could ever describe.

To my four beautiful daughters: Angie, Alyssa, Ashley, and Aimee. You have made me a much better person by being your mama and I am so honored to call you mine. Thank you for always supporting me and for being such strong independent women. I get so much joy from all of you and I could not be more proud. Love you all so much xo. To the men you chose to be our son in laws: Brandon, Patrick, West, and Kevin, how amazing to now have four sons who we have gladly welcomed into our family and who we love so very much. To my grandchildren, you always bring a smile to my face and the love for you all is overwhelming. You keep us young and bring so much joy. Family is number one.

To my sister and her wonderful family. You all are special to me and will forever hold a special place in my heart. Shelly, thank you for always cheering me on and sharing your creative talents with me. Love you so very much xo.

To Sheryl for always being a friend who is excited and truly happy for all I do. For also being encouraging and just plain old loving me. Thank you for always being a call or voicemail away.

Thank you to the students and families of Shared Journeys who I loved being with every day. Even on the hard days, we always found a positive light. I learned so much from all of you and it truly was the best part of my career. You are all special and amazing. To Dani, thank you for entering the field of education and being the next generation of successful educators and for being willing to share your story. From the day I met you, I just knew you were going to be something special and I was right. Keep shining.

To the governing board of Shared Journeys thank you for being a strong force in my life and in the lives of the students and families. Your dedication is beyond anything I have ever imagined. Know you have made a huge impact.

To the foundations who believed in me and the mission and vision of Shared Journeys. Without your financial and personal support, Shared Journeys would not be the amazing place that it is. We could not have accomplished what we have without you! To Mike, our angel in heaven, a special thank you for being the first foundation and person to financially believe in me.

To Joan, a second mom I could not have done this without you. Thank you for guiding me and always just being a call away. To Pam and Kelly, whom I have so much admiration for, thank you for all the support always and for being willing to share your story, which will help so many!

To the amazing staff at Shared Journeys, thank you for your dedication, passion and the laughs and tears. To Jessie, our angel in heaven. You my dear showed grace, dedication, and perseverance. You were my calm. I think of you every day and your line of "Why would you do that to yourself Lisa?" resonates with me often. I feel your presence often, especially when I am having my morning coffee.

To Cathy and Apostle Presbyterian Church for taking us in and letting me create a cozy home for not only our students, but their children in our onsite childcare. You believed in us and helped us be seen. You shared in our joys and in our tears. We are all forever grateful for your love and kindness. Ms. Cathy, your visits were so welcomed each and every day. We looked forward to hearing your laugh in the hallway.

To our community partners. There are so many and you know who you are. You wrapped your arms around us and it made a difference. It does take a village to raise a child. Thank you for being our village.

To the staff in the West Allis/West Milwaukee School District who supported and believed in us, thank you! Your hard work has not gone unnoticed.

About the Author

Lisa Colla is a retired teacher of 34 years. She worked in the West Allis/West Milwaukee School District for her entire career teaching grades 1, 2, 3, reading and then creating Shared Journeys Charter School, a high school for teen parents. Lisa is a product of this district and community as West Allis, WI is her hometown. Shared Journeys is true source of community pride hosting a 100% graduation rate and a daily average attendance of 98% There is an onsite childcare and has graduated 350 plus fathers and mothers from 2010-2022. Lisa was also the founder of Morgan Grove Family Center, an after-school and summer-safe place for students located directly on site in a large subsidized apart-

ment complex. She received numerous awards throughout her career including: The Crystal Apple Award, Teacher of the Year, and the Kohl Teacher and Leadership award. She raised over a million dollars in grant funds to support her high school.

Lisa has supported and mentored new teachers in her years in education as well as educated hundreds of students throughout her career. Many keep in touch and have successful careers and most importantly, are amazing citizens who put family first. Lisa continues to support the alumni and staff of Shared Journeys as well as is involved with many other community programs. Lisa is currently a supervisor for students in the education program at Alverno College.

From a young age, Lisa was positively influenced by her parents who did many of their own home renovations and DIYs. Her parents owned a wood business and weekends were spent at craft fairs. This allowed Lisa to observe creativity and hard work to be successful as well as meet a vast array of creative people. These experiences influenced and supported her love of design. She has taken pride in her home and classrooms and designed the entire school space, school coffeehouse and onsite childcare for Shared Journeys. After college, she married her high school sweetheart and the love of her life, Jeff Colla. They flipped 7 homes all while building their family of four daughters. Most recently they embarked on building their first new build and home of their dreams. Together, they own a small staging business. Although her passions are her faith, education, personal wellness, and design, there is nothing more important than her friends and her family which is always number one. Lisa holds a bachelor's degree in education grades 1-8, health minor grades k-12, reading license grades 1-8, Master's in education, alternative education license, online instructor license, child care certification, and is trained in mindfulness. Lisa's goal is to be her personal best each and every day with always giving back to the community.

About the Contributors

Joan Delaney is a retired educator and administrator for the West Allis/West Milwaukee School District. Joan is passionate about providing learning opportunities for all students and helping remove challenges and barriers to student success. She was a member of the Shared Journey's Governing Board from 2011-2023. Currently, Joan continues her relationship with a former student mentee, her son, and former staff and board members of Shared Journeys. Outside of this role, she gardens, enjoys reading historical fiction books, meets with friends, travels with her husband and cherishes time with her three grown children, their spouses, and 5 grandchildren.

Pam Dowling is a Regional Vice-President with Primerica Financial Services for the past 34 yrs. One of her passions in life, and she has many, is teaching people how money works. She believes that teaching money fundamentals to all would make a marked impact on society. She has been an instructor with Shared Journeys from 2012 - 2023. She was a governing board member from 2018 - 2023. She strives to live her passions out loud by living a faithful life, bringing family and friends together to make more memories, whether it's local or traveling afar, being active swimming, hiking, walking, gardening, creating and reading. She has a full life with her partner and their combined children.

Danielych Heben is a Shared Journeys alumna spending much of her high school career at Shared Journeys who after graduating attended Alverno College and received her Bachelor of Science in Education Degree. Danielych is now a 6th grade teacher for Milwaukee Public Schools. In her spare time she loves spending time with her family, visiting new places and relaxing by watching Netflix. Danielych remains close with her mentor Lisa Colla and she continues her passion of supporting teen parents by volunteering at Shared Journeys.

Kelly Lannoye is the mother of a former Shared Journeys student. Kelly was also a member of Shared Journeys Governing Board. Kelly works full time in healthcare. In her spare time she loves spending time with her parents, husband, children and 6 grandchildren. Kelly enjoys reading and learning, particularly about self improvement and the power of the mind. Kelly is a big advocate for mindfulness and the importance of kindness and positivity in this world. Kelly also enjoys traveling and watching the Packers.

1

Lisa's Story—My Journey to Set Up a School for Teen Parents

Where It All Started

"You are going to do what?" "Why would you do that?" "Aren't you just promoting teen pregnancy by doing this role?" "So you are just going to make it easy for them? They chose this."

Blah blah blah. I had made a big decision to apply for an open position in our school district titled "School Age Parent Teacher." I was at a point in my career as an elementary reading teacher where I needed something else. Something different. A challenge. In reading the job description, I felt like I could check all the boxes and I was fit. I am a mother of four beautiful daughters, have a vast background in child development and early literacy, and am familiar with community resources as I grew up in the community that had the open position. I was a product of this school district I worked in and had been teaching there my entire career. As you can imagine, I applied, interviewed, and was awarded the position. Little did I know the day I received my keys to the school; my life would drastically change.

I met the former teacher for training on teacher orientation day. This "training" consisted of two hours and lunch together. That is it. "Here are your keys, here is your school (which was located in the lower level of an office building—yes the basement), and here are some materials." The previous teacher kept telling me how sorry she felt for me throughout this brief interaction. I kept thinking, "Lady, obviously you don't know me. I love a challenge." Later I would know exactly why she was saying that. There I was, standing in the middle of the classroom, with no co-workers, no curriculum, no assessments, no principal, no support staff, only me-solo, excited and wide-eyed and so the story begins.

On this orientation afternoon, I received a call from one of the local high schools, "Hi we have one for you and need your help. She just told her mother via text that she is expecting and we need you to come here and meet with the student and her mother who is on the way and let them know about your school and how you can help." I told them I would be right there and as I was driving over to the school, I was panicking and thinking what on earth am I going to tell these people. I don't know what I am doing! When I entered the small conference room both mom and daughter were crying. I am not sure exactly why I kicked into gear, but my teacher role and mother role just did. I was empathetic and told them I was there for them both and that we were going to get through this as a team. I remember looking into that student's eyes and the fear was screaming out at me. Then, I looked into her mom's eyes and disappointment was peering back at me. I only hoped when they looked into my eyes, they saw safety and security and not a teacher who had NO idea what she was doing. In this meeting, we created a plan and she did begin attending our school. She is now a confident adult, married, homeowner, and a mother of four. After graduation, I asked her if she could tell I had no clue what I was doing. She said. "Um no Mrs. Colla I did not. You were there for me, listening and willing to help during one of the hardest times in my life so far." She laughed when I told her how nervous I was and that I thought "Well honey, we are going to be learning right next to each other," and that we did.

The first day of school is one I will never forget. My first student to arrive came bopping into the classroom and said, "Are you the new teacher? What kind are you?" I said that I was indeed the new teacher and asked what kind she hoped I was. She said a nice one who cares and teaches good stuff and one that is not as strict as the last teacher. I told her I would do my best. I learned my first lesson that day. Teen parents are selfless. Everything is about their child. In this conversation, the student told me how she was working almost full-time while also going to school along with being a mother to pay the bills. She said she wanted to get a new outfit for school, but all her money had gone for her child so she was wearing the same clothes she wore last year. I told her she looked beautiful. She smiled. The first day was spent chatting with this one student and a few others who sauntered in. The students were unsure of me as the new teacher and wondered what our school would be like. I must have been doing okay because, in October of that year, my classroom was filled with 32 students and grew to 54 in total being serviced in my first year. I learned quickly that the students were my best sales reps.

The days were long. I was teaching four different classes a day, all of which were brand new to me. I created the lessons daily, learning the content right alongside the students. My role was all-encompassing from a teacher, dean, principal, counselor, food service, social media technician, transportation arranger, second mother, birthing coach, and community liaison and I should not forget bathroom cleaner. By Christmas, I completely understood why the former teacher kept saying, "I feel sorry for you." I felt sorry for myself too. There I was at the end of the school day, standing in the middle of our classroom, in tears. What had I done? Could I please go back to teaching reading in elementary school? Feeling defeated, I went home. Sharing with my husband how I was feeling, he said, "Lisa do what you want, but you were never a quitter." He was right. I needed to make this work and that I did.

First was changing my mindset from, what have I done to myself to look at what I am doing and can accomplish. I peered around the classroom looking at each pregnant and parenting high school student and knew they deserved so much more than the judging and uncomfortable feeling of not really fitting in wherever they went. They needed a place that was safe and was considered their home. They needed to know how amazing each and every one was. They needed reassurance that they could do this. They needed parenting support. They needed career support. They needed a quality education. They needed community resources. They needed love. These were the foundations of the school that was to be built. Thus, I began building our school along with the help of so many who jumped on board believing in the mission and vision. This was a school creation that we could be proud of. A school that would graduate 100% of the seniors and have a daily average attendance rate of 98%. A school that students, staff, and the community loved and were proud to be a part of.

2

What Teen Parents Need

As I began to build what was a program into a school, I needed to think about what it is exactly that teen parents need. Oftentimes what they need is exactly what all humans need. As you read each section of what a pregnant or parenting teen needs, you will find the overarching theme is HOPE. Young parents need to know that they are not doomed. Their life can and will go on, but it will just look differently than originally planned. Personal goals can be achieved.

Lending a Listening Ear

My first observation was pregnant and parenting students need someone to listen. They need time to think in a nonjudgmental environment along with having those around them who truly cared. I learned this lesson many times throughout my life, but one that resonates didn't happen with a teen parent or even in our school.

It was Thursday—5:00 PM. I was racing into Walmart right after work to make a return and grab the rolls I needed for dinner. I quickly made my return and determined the route for the fastest way to get to the baked goods. I decided to cut through the shoe section to avoid all the cart traffic near the cash register area.

As I was burning through the shoe area, I was immediately stopped by a large pile of shoes in my way and a woman sitting on a bench. I briefly looked at her and smiled and was about to turn my cart around when she said, "Sorry honey I bet you are wondering why I am just sitting here with a pile of shoes by me." I said, "Oh, no, that is totally fine, no worries at all. I hope you find some comfy ones. " She then stated, " I am here and can't concentrate on anything as my house just burned down and I have nothing to wear." Oh my goodness! I stopped right in my tracks. I told her how sorry I was and we started to chat.

She shared about her insurance company, family, and all that she had lost. My heart just hurt for her. She kept apologizing for taking up my time. Then she said something that I just could not believe. She said, "You are so sweet to stop and talk to me. You are the first person who has just listened to me and I really appreciate you. My dear, you are smiling and so kind, but I can tell you have sadness in your eyes." Well, that is all she needed to say and I was instantly teary and told her that it was amazing to me that a stranger in Walmart could recognize that about me. I then went on to tell her my heart was actually very much hurting as my mom had recently passed away. I also thanked her because she was the first person who had asked how I was feeling that day and who had taken the time to listen. I told her how I very much appreciated her and I shared with her all about my incredible mom. She just listened.

Although this encounter was roughly 15 minutes; It was powerful! I truly believe things happen for a reason. That particular day and in that very moment each of us needed someone to listen. We parted ways saying how each of us wished the best for the other and that we were sending positive vibes between us. As I was checking out, I saw her in the line next to me. She winked at me. I winked back.

The next day, a student asked if she could come by my office after class and if I could help her apply to beauty school. We had done this already together and it seemed strange that she would want to do this again. However, of course, I invited her in. As she was getting logged into her computer, she just reviewed what we had already completed. My Walmart encounter from the previous day started to play in my mind. She just needed me to ask her how she was and listen and that is exactly what I did. She told me all about her Grandma, her mom's upcoming surgery, her fear of leaving our school upon graduation, her confusion about a relationship she was in, and asked about diaper deals. Very little was done regarding college applications. We had already accomplished all of that. As she was leaving my office she said, "It was so great catching up with you Mrs. Colla. I hope we can do this when I graduate." I assured her once part of the family, always part of the family. She just needed me to listen, ask her how her day was, and reassure her that she was always part of the family. The power of asking "How are you?" and then just listening!

I always greeted the students as they walked into the building with, "Good morning! How are you?" I meant that too. I wanted to truly know and would ask to hear. I was listening and they craved that. I knew within seconds what kind of day the student was already having by the reaction to my questions. Sometimes he or she just said "Eh and good morning" and other times "I need to talk." The door of my office was always open and I typically had quite a crew sitting around my long table chatting before school even started. I didn't have all the answers and that was okay. What I did have was the ability to listen and acknowledge that I cared.

Structure

Although many of the students had been fending on their own and going about their days as they pleased, they craved structure. Knowing that our day was consistent and being in the know about what was coming next provided a sense of calm. It was bizarre to me that the students were disappointed when school was closed due to the weather and sad when summer arrived. Although I had graduated from high school a long time ago in 1984, I most definitely remember longing for summer and cheering for a day off school. What was different for me versus my students? I had parents at home who loved me. This is not to say my students did not have family or parents who loved them. However, since they were parents or soon-to-be parents, many were no longer living at home. It was safe at my home growing up and I knew that there was going to be food on the table each night as well as a parent there to talk with. Our bills were paid, our home was clean and I had clothes to wear each day. Although we did not have a lot of money growing up, I knew that I could depend on my family to help me with what I needed. For some of my students, they were no longer on good terms with their parents due to the pregnancy, out on their own, or living in a home shared with a number of family members or friends. Some did not have a bed to sleep in, moving from place to place on a day-to-day basis or living in parks, cars, or wherever they could rest their head. For many, after-school hours were not consistent and were very unpredictable. This created a sense of heightened stress and fear. Due to often couch surfing, the students and their children were involved in unsafe situations. One of my first tough cases I recall was when a male student who had returned from a short prison stay, had been couch surfing and came to school upset that he had applied for a car loan to find out he had poor credit. After further investigating, we found that someone had stolen his social security card and other personal information that he had kept in his wallet. Unfortunately, at one of his many stops, someone decided to take advantage of him. They put all the bills of this particular home in his name. The bills were not being paid and his identity had been stolen. We worked for months to get this resolved. Which immediately had me teaching a lesson on keeping your identity safe and offering any student who was moving from home to home to keep important paperwork locked at school in our safe.

Desiring to have consistency and structure made it very difficult for me to ever be away from school. If I was going to be gone for more than a day, this is the one time I would not inform the students as to when I would be gone. I had found that when I was gone, they were gone. The poor substitutes who covered for me for the very few times I ever missed a school day! They did not like change. Life was unpredictable and stressful so I tried very hard to be present at school.

Dependability

If I said I was going to do something, I had better do it. So many students have been let down by family, friends, the baby's mother or father, society, and the education system. "I will be there for you all the way" was something I truly

meant. At times, there was a bit of shock when the students found that I did mean that and that I was indeed good for my word. One of our new high school fathers had a Friday night parent evening for his football team. No one was going to be there for him. I told him my husband and I would come to the game and be there for him. His response was, "Oh nice, but no you won't." We were there. When his name was called, we cheered and he saw us up in the stands. He looked up in the stands and smiled. On Monday, he said, "Wow you were there." He is now rewriting the story and he is an involved parent and there for his child. I tried to model this over and over.

One of my Latina students truly wanted to go to college. She was 16 and married and her husband wanted her to stay home. She asked if I could come to their apartment and talk with him about college and help her explain why she wanted to attend college. I told her indeed I would and went to their home. We talked and at the end of our conversation, he was not really interested in this idea. A week went by and at the end of our conversation, I set up a college tour for the three of us to attend. Although he was there, he still did not like the idea. We kept at it and eventually, she was enrolled in college. I was someone she could depend on.

Sometimes being dependable is being present. Each morning I arrived early to school to try and get a jump start on the work before staff and students arrived and to read and respond to student journals. We journaled daily. I tried to read and respond on a daily basis. I told students if two days had gone by and I was not responding, please let me know. I also asked students to let me know if their journals needed to be a priority. I remembered how valuable this was when journaling with my own daughters. Kids look for their parents in the audience. High school students are no different. They still look for and hope for their support system in the audience. For many of my students, the journal or before school visits with me were the only opportunities they had for someone to truly listen. I visited their homes, attended plays, football games, volleyball games, and cooking class final projects, stopped by their places of employment, and attended all high school graduations, college graduations, baby showers, and weddings. I was and still am involved in many of their lives. I loved being involved and they knew it. The school-family bonds are important for students to desire to attend.

A student came to class one morning and asked to see me in my office. I noticed what I thought were hickeys all around her neck. As she sat down, she began to cry and soon was crying so hard I could hardly understand what she was saying. After getting her to breathe and calm a bit she stated she had tried to complete a suicide that morning by hanging herself in the basement. I hugged her and told her how grateful I was that she was unsuccessful. I told her I needed to let her mom know that this had happened and that I was going to need to call her. She begged me not to, but I explained I had to as that was my job. I called her mom and she told me that her daughter was dramatic and a faker. I assured her that her daughter was not faking and that she had the marks on her neck to show for it. I explained she would need to get the help she so desperately needed. Her mom stated she would not take her to treatment, but agreed to let me arrange for her daughter to seek treatment. I was able to get coverage for our classroom to be with the other students and I drove this girl home to get her belongings and then drove her to treatment. When we arrived at her home, her mother was lying on the couch and never got up. She just said to her daughter, "Hey are you stupid or something?" I followed her daughter into her room to assure safety and told her she was not stupid. She was in treatment for quite a while. I worried about her returning to that home, but she seemed to manage with the support of our school and therapist. She knew her school and teacher were dependable and we were there for her. Thankfully, her baby was well cared for by a family member while she was in treatment and that was reassuring knowing that she would not lose custody of her child while getting the help she so desperately needed.

Acceptance

One morning a student came bursting through our classroom doors and she was bawling. I asked what was wrong and she stated that the city bus driver had berated her for being a teen and pregnant. The driver must have decided this was first a good decision to share such an opinion like that and to complete this in front of everyone who happened to be riding on the bus. He told her she should be ashamed and that she was a burden to our society. This provided for a great learning opportunity as I decided it was a good idea to call the bus company and respectfully report this behavior in front of the entire school. The students not only saw how to handle an inappropriate situation, but they also witnessed that I believed in them and that everyone deserves to be accepted and respected. Although the student was still mortified, she knew we were family and I had her back.

We lead by example. As a child, one of the first family vacations I can remember was traveling to Mississippi to visit my mom's best friend and her family. I believe I was 5. My parents worked hard to save for this two-week trip. I recall visiting a souvenir shop and purchasing a large conch shell with money my grandma had given me. I was told I could hear the ocean in that shell if I listened carefully and to my amazement I could! I wanted more in the gift shop at the time and my parents told me that the money I had was used for the shell so I would not be able to get the other items. This lesson is so valuable for any child or teen to learn. You just can't always have what you want when you want it and that your life is full of choices. I chose my shell just like my students had chosen to parent their child. Sometimes they had to wait to have the new diaper bag, purchase a car or get a babysitter to spend time with friends and that was just fine.

My parents were very good at sticking to what they believed. Besides the conch shell, there are other memories that I have from this trip that left lasting impressions on me and I believe have helped mold me into who I am today. Life experiences that then I shared with my students.

We were on the beach and playing in the sand. My mom and dad were helping my sister and me build a sand castle. Suddenly, we heard screaming. A lady was asking for help as her two young daughters were in the water and the tide was pulling them out farther and farther. They could not get back to the shore. My dad never hesitated, raced into the water, swam out to the young girls, and brought them both to shore. I remember watching him thinking he is truly the strongest person in the world. His military background and swimming abilities from swimming around my grandparents' lake as a child made this second nature for him. The girls were safe and their mother was incredibly grateful. Then yet another memory I have of our trip is that we were made to head down into the cellar. A tornado was on the way. As we all huddled together singing songs like "This Land is Your Land" and I was learning to spell "Mississippi" to help ease the fear, a roar began to hum. It became louder and louder and then, it sounded like a train was directly over us. It was loud and scary! I remember clinging to my mom. Once the sound disappeared, we slowly made our way out of the cellar. To our great joy, there was little damage to the home we were staying at. A few trees were down and that was about the extent of it. However, a car pulled into the driveway, and a man came running up to us. He said the tornado had hit the mobile home park up the road and they were in dire need of help. This was a trip my parents had saved for to have relaxation and fun and yet, off my dad went. Once again, there was never a hesitation. He was gone for what seemed like hours. When he arrived, he was full of dirt and looked tired. He told us that he helped some small children out of their overturned home that they had been trapped underneath. I know there was a lot more to that story as he was off whispering about it with my mom. Their philosophy was that little people don't need to worry about big people's problems. I agree! The good news is I went to bed that night after again witnessing my father helping someone in need. I saw that many times throughout my years growing up from both of my parents. How fortunate I have been.

I learned at a very young age to help when needed and speak kindly to others. I was shown to help your neighbor. Give up your seat so someone older or more in need can have it. Never make fun of others. Be respectful saying, "please," "thank you," "nice to meet you," "I am sorry," and to be a listener, just to name a few. My husband and I have worked to raise our family in the same way. I have now had the joy of watching our adult daughters treating others with respect, compassion, helping whenever possible, and participating in volunteer opportunities, along with raising a family.

Unfortunately, helping others is not always the case for those in our society. My husband and I were recently enjoying an ice cream at a local restaurant. Seated around us were many tables filled with adults and children along with some teenagers. From afar, we saw an elderly woman walking toward the tables. She fell and could not get up. Not one person stopped what he or she was doing to help. They clearly saw, took a look, and continued to eat their hamburgers, and ice cream, and look at their phones. My husband raced over to help her up, get seated, and be sure she was okay. She was so grateful and clearly shaken. I stood in complete disbelief. Was this really happening? Not one person would even think of helping? Really? I could hear my dad's voice ringing in my ears, "Get up, we need to get over there and help that poor lady." At that very moment, it didn't matter what political party anyone was in and it didn't matter what race anyone was. It didn't matter who was rich or poor or what was on the social media feed on many of the phones that were out that day. What did matter was being a good human. We ALL lead by example. Those children and teens just witnessed their parents or the adults they were with do absolutely nothing to help. I am hopeful they watched my husband and learned. We can support each other to be our personal best and I truly believe that we can ALL do better!

It was a choice to attend our school. We were one of the five high schools in our city. Typically, the counselors at the comprehensive high schools would call and state they had a student they would like for me to come by and meet with as he or she was going to be a parent or transferred into our school district and was a parent. I would head to the school and meet with the student to explain about my role, our school and highlight that we were a school family. We would then make a plan for a transfer if the student chose to attend our school. Some students were too early in their pregnancy to transfer as we did not complete a transfer until the students were 12 weeks pregnant, but I would continue to visit him or her at their comprehensive high school to begin teaching about pregnancy and parenting. I was building a relationship with the student and the student was feeling seen and heard. To be honest, I never had a student who declined coming to our school. Being a pregnant teen in high school is difficult. It is hard to relate to other teens who are concerned about things like getting to the football game and shopping while being pregnant brings many worries such as: where the money will come from to purchase diapers, childcare while at work, and doctor appointments along with physical and emotional changes. People are talking about them and there are endless looks. They feel like an alien. Their friends that they once had are often not too interested in hanging out with them and sometimes their friend's parents do not want them interacting with the "pregnant kid" any longer. There are problems within their family with shame, sadness, remorse, anxiety, and anger. They need a place to feel accepted and a place that they can relate to their classmates. Our school provided that. They were accepted, respected, and loved. Our school was filled with wonderful students who were willing to be a friend and help in any way possible. They all witnessed giving back and they all understood how important it was to stick together and just plain old help each other out.

Fun

The parenting teens need fun. They are teens with a developing teen brain, trying to live in an adult world. Now this is not to say that the adult world is not fun. However, fun as an adult often looks different than fun as a teen. The students are now responsible for this little human along with themselves. So, at our school, we started by laughing all the time. I shared funny stories, the students were able to share often and I always tried to have something for them to look forward to. Due to the grant writing that I completed each year, we went on many full-paid field trips to get out of the classroom and into the world to provide an authentic learning experience. I selected trips that would

let the students explore and try new things. One of the trips we attended on a yearly basis was to go to the Betty Brinn Children's Museum for a tour and parenting class. This in turn would afford the students a free membership to the museum. After this tour, we would go out to lunch at the Milwaukee Public Market. Table manners were taught and no cell phones were allowed to be out while eating. This pushed the students to have conversations while having proper etiquette. Some would question why their phones could not be out. I would explain that they were retraining their brain to have a conversation rather than texting their thoughts. It was incredibly difficult for some to do this. We considered it a challenge. Another trip we went on yearly was to Discovery World Museum in Milwaukee, after to Colectivo Coffee House, and then for a walk along Lake Drive. I knew instantly this was an appropriate trip for high school students when the first time we took this trip, a student asked me if the water we were seeing was the ocean. Now mind you our city is 30 minutes south of Lake Michigan. I replied with, "No, actually this is Lake Michigan." The student said, "Oh, wow, I have never seen this." I replied, "So glad you have so you can be sure you are taking your baby here to explore." I learned to never assume anything. Going to the pumpkin farm and Milwaukee County Zoo, shopping at the Farmer's Market to then make a recipe with the food purchased, attending college visits and job shadows were novel experiences for so many and incredibly necessary. My staff and I planned monthly family nights. Some were at school in the evening or on the weekend and some were even via Zoom. Alumni were invited to these as well. We have a strong alumni base who have an allegiance to our school. Having current students mixed in with alumni provides learning and role models. One of the large events each year was Santa Saturday in which the students come to school with their child, receive a picture with Santa, have treats and each child receives a gift. Local banks and churches provide these gifts. The Easter Egg Hunt is another favorite. The joy of watching children of all ages running around looking for eggs! In the summer is our annual gathering in the park. There is so much conversation with students both current and alumni. Feeling a part of something, and how wonderful to belong.

A school district administrative staff member was questioning the fact that I would take students on all of these trips FREE of charge. She said other students were not privy to this. My reply, "These aren't other students, they are my students and I am making sure that they have learning that is fun and meaningful. Not a dime is coming out of school district fund for these trips. This is all from grant funding, fundraisers, and community donations." So many are on board supporting us from funding, to mentoring, to providing basic needs. This individual stopped questioning.

Leveling of the Playing Field

-Mladen Zivkovic/Shutterstock.com

"I am not going to prom. I can't afford the tickets or a dress." Well, that was not acceptable in our school family. This student's mentor along with many generous community members helped me to get anyone to prom who so desired. We helped this student with a dress as I gave her one of my daughter's dresses. A friend came by school one day and altered the dress. Her mentor purchased prom tickets for her and an alumni did her makeup and hair on the day of prom. This was common. We all worked together to get anyone what he or she needed. Another student could not get to school as her car was needing so many repairs. I contacted our auto shop teacher and explained the situation. Her car became an auto class project and was repaired for her to get back and forth to school. Never once did a student at our school need to purchase supplies or even pay for anything. Everything was provided. No student needed to feel as though he or she was less than. We created milestone scrapbooks and all supplies including printing pictures were taken care of. This modeling then carried over to the students in that if they had something more than another, they would share. Food was always available and the students could graze all day. This was a necessity as some had little to no food at home and coming to school was a way to get their nutritional needs met. We had clothes for the students and personal hygiene products. There were students who brushed their teeth each morning upon arriving at school. We had a "boutique" for baby clothes. The community and students would donate clothing that was no longer needed. Students could shop between classes or before and after school. I was questioned if the students "abused" this system. My response, "No, why would they?" They certainly never did. They took what they needed and not anymore. Most would donate back to the boutique after their child had grown out of what they had shopped for. The holidays were especially hard for a number of our students, so Christmas presents were collected from local businesses and community partners, and Thanksgiving meals were provided for those in need. Graduation fees were paid for those who needed it and caps and gowns were purchased. I hosted a Senior Luncheon each year. Students felt celebrated and special. We went to a fancy restaurant and they could order any meal off the menu. Even dessert which was a BIG deal! Each received a personal hand written card from me and gifts. In fact, I even was known to steam gowns at school before heading to graduation. We had a weekly food pantry on site in which all students could bag up groceries they would use and take them home to whomever they were living with. Letters of recommendation were created and personal statements were written in school and support was given for editing. College applications were filled out at school and any fees paid.

Helping teens unlock the mystery of parenting and child development was simply delightful. Since I am personally passionate about both subjects, it was exciting to support the journey. My hope was that I was a person the students felt comfortable with to share. Students often hung around after school and sadly some had no desire to head home. This is also when they would tend to ask for something they may need. One student in particular took food daily. His mom had recently passed and his father was not in a good state of mind. I gave him healthy snacks to take home. One day he stopped and came back into the room and said, "Mrs. Colla, can I have some extra food? My brother is hungry too." Oh my! My heart literally sank. I think I gave him the whole box of granola bars that night and gave him extras from there on out. I still get text messages to this day from this student. He checks in and tells me how life is for him as well as wants to know how I am doing. As educators, we need to constantly be seeking ways to creatively level the playing field.

Resources

polinaloves/Shutterstock.com

"Will it hurt when I deliver?" I would always reply, "You know I will not lie to you. Yes, it will hurt. However, remember that this is only temporary and you get a beautiful baby at the end." One of my alumna reminded me of how she delivered without pain medication chanting, "This is only temporary." Students were able to partake in a child development 1 and 2 course as well as a prenatal course at school. Within these courses, the students learned about children's development and the parental role from birth to age one, as well as in the toddler years from ages one to three. In addition, the prenatal course educated students on their changing body, how to care for themselves, labor and delivery, breastfeeding, nutrition and bringing a new baby home.

On site, we had a clinical psychologist who would meet with students on a weekly basis. Students could sign up to see him. They loved being able to talk through their life challenges with such a wise and trusted individual. The value of this was incredible. Not only to have accountability to try what was suggested and then come back and report how things went, but also to have someone to collaborate and brainstorm with. It was so nice that there was never any pressure to meet. If a student just was not feeling it that day, he or she did not need to meet. There also was no judging.

We were connected with many community support services that were willing to help our school. Local colleges formed partnerships with us visiting our school and offering tours. The goal was to have students prepared for the next steps in life. They needed to know about community resources and we shared all we knew from the local health department for vaccinations to finding physicians and dentists that matched their insurance. We visited food banks and shared where to find diapers if needed. Brainstorming and organizing were crucial as we wanted students to have the knowledge to plan ahead.

Sometimes the students needed safety. Our school was a exactly this during the day. Gangs, drugs, poverty and homelessness was nothing new for us or a number of our students. This also meant helping the students to be safe outside of school. Housing was often an issue. One day a student came into school upset and asked if she could talk to me. She was clearly scared. I asked what was upsetting her and she told me she had moved away from her grandmother's home due to constant disagreements and was living in an old vacated building that had no heat or electricity. She was fearful that she and her baby would get bit from the rats and cockroaches filling up the premises. Her only source of heat and electricity was from her neighbor who was kind enough to let her run extension cords from his home to hers so that she could have a space heater and a lamp running. As you can imagine, my heart was breaking and by that night she was living in a safe space. We were able to get her into a local shelter until she was able to eventually work things out with her grandmother. Many students became homeless and were living in trap houses, parks, public bathrooms, cars, under park benches and couch surfing from home to home. Sharing resources of safe living was a top priority and we did all we could to get students a safe place to sleep each night not only themselves, but their child as well.

Though the years I had many students who lost parents or family members to drug addiction. Sadly, one day that resonates with me is while on a field trip, my phone was ringing. Since we were on the bus, I answered the call as it was from a student from the year before. I could hardly understand what she was saying through the tears and screams besides "He is dead" Both she and her baby's father had attended our high school as seniors. Her baby's father struggled to be at the comprehensive high school in our school district and since he was going to be a father, he was invited to attend our school along with his pregnant girlfriend. Our school was his last hope to graduate. We were all so proud on graduation day. The picture of the two of us with him in his graduation cap and gown will forever be a favorite of mine. The big smile on both of our faces. This was not an easy road to get him to graduation. He was such a wonderful person, but he struggled with drug use and abuse. His family along with our school offered many support services to help him to sobriety. Unfortunately, he was unable to stay clean and overdosed on heroin driving into an electrical pole. The day this happened our school filled with alumni needing support. We all were together that day and at the funeral. A true school family that stuck together

Strong Academics

"How unfortunate. You had a bright future." "It is a bummer that now you won't be able to follow your dreams." "College is not really an option for you. What type of job are you thinking about?" True statements said directly to the pregnant and parenting teens. So motivational right? Wrong! When the students came to our school, they were asked what they would like to do after

high school. Looking either confused or defeated, I would explain that they can do anything they would like and that the path may just look a little different to getting there. For example, I had a student who wanted to go to an art school in California. She did go to college for art, but stayed in Wisconsin which was closer to home for support with her child while in school. We had many speakers come to our school and discuss their careers. Some had been teen parents themselves and were now through post-secondary training. Students wrote a personal statement to now prepare for applying for college and scholarships. We helped students fill out the FAFSA, informed them of scholarships to apply for, went on college tours and each student participated in a job shadow of choice. I know first hand how powerful a job shadow can be. Had I been given this opportunity as a high school student, I may not have spent a year in nursing school only to switch to teaching after realizing during my first round of clinical experience that this career was not for me! Having the opportunity to take parenting courses, career courses, prenatal courses, financial literacy, yoga, and mindfulness, along with academic courses helped support the students to meet success in their futures. There was choice built in each course so students could create their own path to meet the learning targets. Since I was a former reading teacher, I made sure to not only help students to realize the importance of reading to their baby even before delivery but to continue reading to their child on a daily basis. Teaching to have books everywhere was a priority. We had students who were struggling and credit deficient to students who were taking advanced placement courses. It was imperative to have individual learning plans for each student. They were involved in their plans creating academic, social, and personal goals. These goals were reviewed quarterly, but more often if needed. We had a school lending library for the high school students. They were able to take any book of interest and just return when completed. It was an honor system that worked. We always ended up with more books than we started with. That is because the students would bring other books that they so loved and wanted to share with others. We also had a lending library for the high school students' children. This was filled with books. We were able to keep this full with the support of our community donating books and also organizing book drives for our school.

Barriers Removed

Our school was a welcoming place. Basic needs were being met at school which was such a necessity for many students. Food, clothing, a safe space, transportation, and childcare were all part of our school support system. A washer and dryer were provided to allow students to wash their own personal clothing if they were living in transition or between homes. Transportation was also provided. Students were able to receive bus tickets as well as a school district cab if they needed a ride to school. A student needed to have strong attendance to receive a week's worth of bus tickets, but a newer student or one having some attendance issues received one ticket a day to get from home to school with eventually earning a week's worth of tickets. One of our most difficult barriers was childcare. In our first years creating the school, we helped students secure childcare outside of the school and if that was not a possibility, students would bring their child to school. This was the best we could do at the time so as to not have students missing school. As you can imagine the disruptions and distractions were rampant. The goal was to create on-site childcare. After writing many grants to be turned down, one foundation, came to support us which led us to another and another. All were incredibly generous and in 2018, we were able to open our on-site childcare. This was a huge undertaking not only creating a beautiful and welcoming child care center in our building that accommodated children 3 weeks to 4 years old, but also being sure that our staff was child care certified. This involved taking coursework to become certified as well as once certified to have continued education opportunities. In addition, we had to install extra security to be sure the children in the childcare were safe. We also helped students find out their insurance possibilities for medical, dental, and vision not only for themselves but also for their child. This then leads to finding a doctor for their personal needs. Those who needed employment would receive support in applying with interview practice, letters of recommendation, and going shopping at Goodwill to find interview clothing.

Flexibility

Assignments were not optional, they were mandatory. Even though the students were parents or soon-to-be parents, that did not excuse them from completing the course requirements. However, what was allowed was flexibility. If a student had a newborn and was up all night, an assignment may be approved to be turned in the day after the assignment was due. If a student had a doctor's appointment or her child was sick, she could work from home and turn in her schoolwork in our Google classroom. Zoom meetings and before and after school help was provided. We also provided mentors both for educational purposes as well as life skills support. Learning to be a parent and manage work, life, and school was what we were helping to teach so that the students could stand on their own once they left our school. Love and understanding were always part of the daily routine. Even if a student was not happy about having to complete this work, she knew there was a reason I would ask her to complete it. With such strong and mutually respectful relationships built at our school, disrespect and negative behaviors were just not a problem.

Giving Back To

LightField Studios/Shutterstock.com

The students were incredibly grateful for all of the support that they received. One way that they gave back was to create an outdoor food pantry that was stocked daily. Similar to our free lending outdoor library, this was an outdoor boxed area where residents of the community could come by and take whatever they needed. It was stocked with canned goods, cereal, baby items, and other food staples. The food to stock this daily was from community donations. The community could drop food off for us to fill the food pantry on a daily basis, or they could also just fill the food pantry as they drove by. From the young mom walking her children by our school each morning in a tattered stroller, to the high school student, like a sleuth quickly grabbing something each day on his way home from school so as to not let anyone see he needed food, to the elderly woman who walked up to the pantry rain or shine to put food in to share. This became a loved party of our community. One day I received a call from my friend and the pastor of the church to inform me that our pantry had been ruined. It seemed that a resident who was not mentally well, smashed the pantry since there was not a food item that she desired. We were devastated. The damage was shared on Facebook and the next day, when we returned to school, we had a new pantry. Residents quickly rebuilt the pantry!

One of the most valued pieces of our school was volunteering at a local nursing home. The students would talk with the residents, enjoy a snack, and play bingo for prizes. Yes, high school students were equally as excited as the residents. In the years that we volunteered, friendships were built and an incredible amount of learning for both the residents and the students magically transpired. The students typically did not have a lot of volunteer experiences under their belts, so this was also a great way to add to their personal resumes for college and scholarship applications as well as employment opportunities. A true win-win situation for all!

Each year, our students were involved in a presentation to the comprehensive high school freshman classes. The title of our program was "The Not So Glamorous Life of a Teenage Parent." This was an incredibly emotional presentation in which our students would pour their hearts out about what life was really like for a teen parent. They started with the idea that yes their babies are so cute on social media, but the reality is life is tough. They shared about being up all night long, losing friends and family members who either are disappointed in them or who are too busy to spend time with them any longer, the financial struggles, relationship issues, and missing out on all the fun a "normal" high school student was involved in. This typically evoked strong emotions and our students ended up crying while telling their stories. Now this was not all sad as the students shared what they were most proud of as a parent and also shared what they were doing to achieve their personal goals. You could hear a pin drop in the auditorium as the other students were listening so intently.

Etiquette

One thing that was nonnegotiable in our school was the expectation of handwriting a thank you card for anything that was received. It seems to be such a lost art that has such an incredible impact. Let's face it, when you show gratitude it is the gift that keeps on giving. You feel good and the person receiving this piece of thanks also feels valued. This was a common practice and I still receive thank you cards and messages from alumni and their children. They are carrying on this positive habit with their families.

Please, thank you, you are welcome, good morning, have a great day, nice to meet you: All taught on a daily basis. This was taught and modeled for me as a child and I did the same for my own children. However, not all families are the same and these were some proper etiquette norms that some students needed to learn. I would catch myself often saying, "Oh what I think you meant to say was, thank you!"

When a new student arrived, we got in a big circle and each of us completed an introduction. We were a family and this needed to be shown from day one on. The students welcomed anyone new with open arms. Many had been outcasts themselves and felt less than in their previous school experiences, so being welcomed was new. To this day, many alumni get together for play dates with their children along with providing support to each other in their adult lives.

Never take more than you need was modeled so students knew that they were privy to daily hygiene products, food, and clothing. We often received donations and the students could take what they needed. I would hear students saying, I only need one loaf of bread for my family so you take two. I would often bring things in for students in need like clothing, food, and even towels. I would say it was just extras at my house that I did not need. Modeling the skill to give is so powerful. They always brought clothing back that no longer fit them or their child to share with others. I did have a couple of students who through the years seemed like they were hoarding anything we had, taking such large amounts home. That was a sign to see what was going on. With further investigation, it was found that the student was trying to feed or clothe the entire family. This was a cry for help and I was able to help with these essentials for families.

The students learned that if they were to be respected, they would need to also show respect. They were all too aware that they were not always seen in a positive light in the community. They also knew that it was imperative that they show class and proper etiquette as they happened to be more scrutinized. A sad, hard truth. Being "ambassadors or knowledge" about many topics such as parenting, mindfulness, prenatal care, child development, and nutrition, they often shared their information learned with family and friends. However, as they were also taught, you can bring a horse to the water, but cannot make the horse drink the water. They understood not everyone has the same beliefs or is willing to listen and try. So being respectful while planting the seed was necessary. A principal that I knew happened to be out with his family at dinner. One of my students saw him as she too was out with her son for dinner. She noticed that his entire family was on cell phones or iPads. She walked over to the table and on her way out said, hello as the principal knew who she was and then went on to tell him that she had learned in school to be present with her child and to put away phones at the dinner table. She then told the family to have a good dinner and left. The principal called me the next day and said, "I had an interesting run-in with one of your students. She saw that my entire family was on technology while out to eat and she did a friendly reminder that this was not helping our family connect. Although at the time I was irritated, I thought about it and she was totally right. Great job teaching the students how to be present with their family." I did have to giggle and said I would talk with her about maybe not calling someone out in public but thinking of a more private way of doing this. Powerful stuff!

If you are school-hunting as a student, parent, employee, or community member who is looking for a place to support below is a checklist of things to consider as you are working through your personal journey. You deserve the best!

Staff

- Are the staff qualified? How do they interact with their students?
- What is their experience?
- Are they fully trained?
- Are they available for after-hour support?
- Are they present and excited to be at school?

Students

- Do they seem invested?
- Are they at the school by choice?
- Are family events well attended?

Statistics

- What are the graduation rates?
- What are the attendance rates?
- What is the post-secondary acceptance rate?
- What are the behavioral rates such as expulsion, and referrals?

Location

- Is the school on a bus line?
- Is this school in close proximity to getting to school on time?

Supports

- Is childcare provided?
- Is flexibility built in?
- Is transportation provided if needed?
- Basic needs support
- Materials provided
- Scholarship support
- FAFSA support
- Employment support
- Clothing (for students and children)
- Food provided
- State assistance support
- Field trips paid
- Career investigation
- Community support and events shared

Succession Plan

Some final thoughts for you all. For the teen parents, you are the reason! You are amazing and you have got this! For the staff working with teen parents know that you're creating a space filled with hope and joy for so many who felt hopeless and confused. For the children, know that you are loved and your parents are doing all they can to be their personal best to raise you. To the community programs, thank you and thank you and thank you! You help a low-budget school be successful with your sharing of talents and resources. To school districts who support teen parents, you are incredible as you are truly putting the student first. To the funders, bless you! You believe in the mission and vision and understand that everyone deserves a quality education. To the grandparents/parents, thank you for still loving your child and grandchild through some very trying times. Our school is such a gift and I not only taught but learned every single day even on my last day before retiring. I have since retired from my role as Program Facilitator and Teacher. Thirty-three years in education and so many precious and powerful memories. I am still involved with our school and am helping to mentor the new staff as well as supporting the transition to a new location.

My advice to anyone working in this capacity is to have a true succession plan in place for when a key employee is going to retire. This does not mean a plan that is taken lightly or discussed minimally placing trust in the idea that the key players understand the daily happenings of the school, but a plan that is discussed at great length and one that is set in stone so that everyone can agree on it Be sure that each piece of the puzzle is covered and that everyone holds a piece to that puzzle. Allow for a transition and training period to happen so that the new staff can become acclimated to a very unique environment. I suggest at least a year of mentoring and training. This way a smooth transition can occur and the school can continue to thrive even in the absence of the previous leader. Change is tough, but it can be successful.

3

Dani's Story: I am Pregnant Now What?

I grew up in a very strict household. Strict, especially for us girls. My mom was a single mom after leaving my dad due to his drug addiction. They made the decision to move to the United States from Puerto Rico, two weeks after I was born. My mom worked a lot so we had to become very independent from a young age. We would be in charge of setting alarms, waking up, getting ourselves dressed, and walking to our bus stop to get to school every day. When we'd get home, my sister and I were in charge of cleaning and making sure we took out the meat so it would be thawed when my mom got home. As girls, we were responsible for most of the household chores and had very limited freedom. We weren't allowed to go over to our friends' houses or hang out with our friends unless they came over to our house. My mom was afraid my sister and I would get pregnant at a young age just like she did.

I met my boyfriend when I was 12 years old. He lived across the street and don't ask me how but I actually found him on social media and sent him a request. We started talking every day, and we would see each other here and there when my mom would let me go over to my cousin's house. My mom found out about us dating and confronted me. She was really upset, she thought I was too young, but she also knew I was hard-headed. I really didn't care what she thought, I was going to date him regardless of her wishes. That was the first time I ever saw my mom be a bit lenient. She told me she would allow me to see him only after she and my stepfather met him. After meeting him they assigned me days of the week in which my boyfriend could come over, they even gave him rides home and picked him up.

At 14 years old, I found myself in the situation my mom was so afraid her daughters would get themselves into if she wasn't as strict as she was. Yes, I was pregnant. To make matters worse, my sister and I would find ourselves in that situation at the same time. Yes, my sister was pregnant. With my sister being pregnant at the same time as I was, it caused me to not tell my mom about my pregnancy for 5 months. I hid it! Watching and hearing my mom so stressed and sad about my sister's pregnancy caused me not to have the heart to tell her about mine. I didn't want to cause my mom any more heartache. I finally had the courage to tell her at my annual check-up. I didn't know how else to tell her and knowing a doctor would be present in the room made me feel brave enough to do so. My mom was upset, sad, angry, and disappointed. I was only 14. How can her baby be having a baby right now? Her baby with such a bright future. Her baby enjoyed going to school and loved to learn. Her baby whose life was just starting.

I was scared. I knew I wanted to finish school, but didn't know how I would do it. I didn't know how I would take care of a baby. I knew I would be judged and the other students at school would talk about me and they did! I was anemic, I had severe nausea, I couldn't sleep and I was missing a lot of school. Missing a lot of school led me to get a truancy ticket.

The first I ever heard about Shared Journeys School was through my sister. She was pregnant and going to a school for teen parents, but that's all I knew. I met Lisa Colla for the very first time when she was called to come to the comprehensive high school and talk with me. I was getting a truancy ticket. I didn't know who she was, I just knew she was there and so understanding and wanting to help. After getting my truancy ticket, a meeting with Mrs. Colla was arranged. I remember her being sweet, and she was the first person I met who didn't look at me with judgment, but with empathy and she just oozed with hope. She knew what I was going through and wanted to help in any way she could. She told me all about Shared Journeys and assured me that if I could trust the process I would graduate. Well, that is what I did. I bought in and had trust in the process. I completed my freshman year and passed all of my classes! That summer I went to Shared Journeys and grabbed all the forms I needed to sign up for Shared Journeys. Every year Mrs. Colla had an individualized plan for me and all of the other students. It was everything we needed to graduate. We just had to follow the process and everything was going to be okay. Over the years I met so many new people. I became friends with other students just like me. I met people who wanted to help and educate me. I met people who cared about me, my daughter, and our future.

Mrs. Colla changed my life. She gave me hope when no one else could. I trusted her and she didn't let me down. Because of Mrs. Colla, I decided to become a teacher. I wanted to be everything she was to me for my future students. I thought everyone deserves to have a Mrs. Colla in their life. After graduating high school I enrolled at Alverno College. Mrs. Colla was there every step of the way from going to my financial aid meeting to editing lesson plans, to providing suggestions, to just listening. She also gave me a job at Shared Journeys where I worked all the way through college. I continued to learn from Mrs. Colla while having such a flexible schedule. I was able to be an academic tutor of the new teen moms coming into our school. I gained tons of teaching experience from Mrs. Colla. I got to work side by side with her and she taught me as much as she could and was my guide through college since I was also a first-generation college student. I graduated college in May of 2023 at the age of 22 with my Bachelor of Arts in Education. I am now a first-year teacher, teaching 6th grade, homeowner, mom of 2 beautiful children and I am still with my boyfriend that I met at 12! Dreams can come true!

My advice for any teen parents or families who are in this situation is to find a Mrs. Colla. Find a school that allows flexibility, reduces barriers, and provides you with every single opportunity to be successful. Surround yourself with people who are like-minded and have goals. This may mean that you need to step aside from relationships that you once had. Those can be memories as you need to put your child first. You can be successful and have the life that you want for you and your child. It is definitely hard work, but it will pay off.

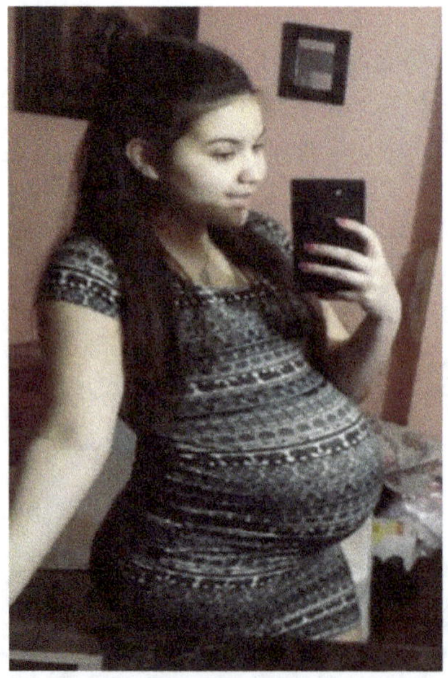

Dani pregnant age 14

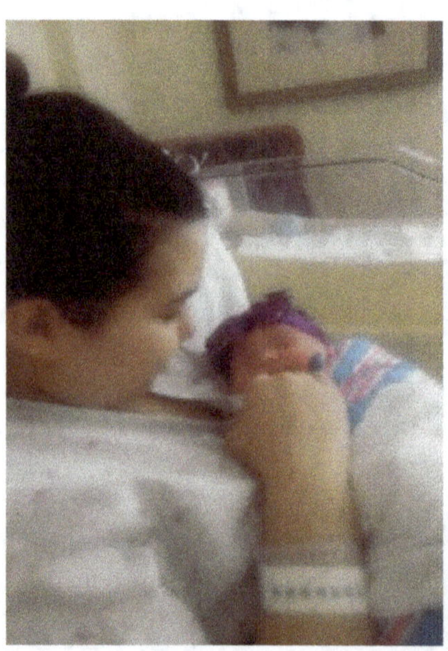

Dani is in hospital after her daughter's birth.

Dani and Mrs. Colla high school

Dani and Mrs. Colla college graduation. Alverno College

Dani's college graduation with her daughter.

4

Kelly's Story: My Daughter Is Pregnant!

I always remember quite vividly the scene in Terms Of Endearment when Shirley MacClain is told she is going to be a Grandmother. She is shocked and screams, "What makes you think I want to be a GRANDMOTHER!"

At 42 and with my 16-year-old telling me she was pregnant...those were my thoughts exactly.

Going back our family is probably now quite the "typical" blended family. I brought into my marriage two girls Alex and Ari. My husband brought a son and daughter, Nick and Kayla.

My girls and I did the "single mother" life for 7 years with no real father figure involved prior to meeting my husband. When my husband Kevin entered the picture the girls took to him right away as he did to them. At 13 and 6, they suddenly had a dad in the home.

During the first few years, the kids all went through their changes and challenges as we adjusted to this new blended family. Alex, 13, the oldest was probably somewhat defiant or maybe I was just harder on her because she was my oldest. Alex never lacked "boyfriends" and most of her friends were boys. Nick, 8, struggled socially and we eventually found out he had Asperger's Syndrome. Nick was very difficult at times and yet really kept to himself a lot. Ari, 6, was into her girlfriends and playing with her baby dolls. (She has always been very maternal).

Kayla, 2 years old, lived with her mother, so we only had her on weekends. It was a great joy having a little toddler in the house on the weekends.

As the kids grew older, I always worried about Alex and again her constant "boyfriends." We made the decision for Alex to go on birth control young, as I was determined to not have any "surprises" in my life.

Ari, on the other hand, joined the pom pon team at school and loved it. Ari developed slowly, and boys were never a concern. Around 14 years old, Ari met Tyler. We didn't get to know him too well as their "dating" seemed more of an "at school" thing.

Alex and Ari have always been my Ying and Yang. Such opposites on so many levels. As Ari and Tyler began "dating," I was still very focused and concerned with Alex.

Alex was beyond book smart and even common sense smart but they sure loved hanging out with only boys! Ari was very involved with activities, with her girlfriends and her studies.

Alex was always mature for her age and Ari was maybe a little immature. Again, Ying and Yang.

Around 15 you could tell Ari was getting pretty attached to Tyler. I remember having some concerns but thought it would pass. There wasn't a lot of time outside of school for the two of them. Birth control wasn't even discussed as I truly couldn't fathom sex being an issue with these two (wrong).

I remember the night when Ari was 16 and there was just a lot of drama going on in the house. Kevin worked nights so it was me home with three kids. Two teenage girls and a teenage boy who pretty much kept to himself with his video games. I don't know the specifics of what exactly was said, but I remember talking with Ari as things were just seeming really off. She was very emotional and loud. Somehow through the course of the drama, it came out she was pregnant. Shocked was an understatement. Again, I don't remember specifics, but clearly remember her going downstairs to her room and me feeling like the house had just fallen on me. Sitting alone unable to breathe.

The next few weeks were a blur. I remember missing work a few times as I was mentally unable to function. I felt depressed, overwhelmed and like a failure of a parent. The flood of emotions was so hard to handle.

I also remember Tyler coming over one night and speaking with him. I didn't know if I should be mad at him or feel sorry for him. He had not yet told his parents and I said he needed to ASAP.

Neither Tyler nor Ari had a strong opinion about the pregnancy as I truly believe they were still children themselves. As shocked as I felt, I believe they were too! Then add in a little denial and naivety.

The time finally came when Heather and Larry, Tyler's parents, were told about the pregnancy. I remember having a phone conversation with them that in my mind did not go well. They were very adamant that these children could not be parents. I couldn't agree more, but also knew there were huge life-altering and moral decisions to be made and I had no clue WHO was going to be the one to make this decision. In my mind Ari and Tyler were children and yet they were now really "parents." And as far as us four parents of these children, it was very clear we didn't see eye to eye.

Kevin was raised Catholic and from the very beginning never had any other thought that this child would be born. Kevin even mentioned at one point we could adopt the baby and take full responsibility, letting Ari and Tyler off the hook in a sense. I couldn't agree or even fathom that option at all, as much as I admired Kevin's wanting to take responsibility for our child.

I have always believed abortion was a woman's choice. Not ever a choice for me personally, but I could never judge a woman who did make that choice. This situation though was completely different because I had my own CHILD of 16 having to make this decision and truthfully as her parent, I felt morally and legally responsible for her decision. She was a child, so could she make the right decision and should she make that final decision? This is a place I wish no parent to ever be in. This weighed on my heart and soul so heavily.

I recall many talks with Ari explaining the ramifications of the choice she made. I explained that as a family we supported her 100% either way. She was always very sure she wanted to have the baby, but I always wanted to make sure she was making the right decision for the right reasons.

Tyler's parents continued to voice their opinions against this pregnancy which just added so much more stress to this all.

At some point, pretty early into the pregnancy, it was decided Ari would keep the baby and as a family, we would support her. I know we even told Tyler's parents we expected no help or support from them, as this was ultimately our family's decision. Which also made me think long and hard about a "father's" say in pregnancy.

Then still pretty early into the pregnancy, Tyler broke up with Ari. This was a whole new level of stress now. Our families were clearly not on the same page about the pregnancy when our kids were dating. This only added more tension between our families.

It became very apparent Ari was very attached to Tyler, maybe too attached, and probably in her young teenage mind this pregnancy was going to bond them forever. She was heartbroken and began to question the pregnancy.

I think any parent of a teenager can agree they all struggle to some degree with mental illness or even mental instability at times during the teenage years. This was definitely the case. Ari was an emotional wreck. Was it hormones? Was it her age? Was it hereditary? I had no clue, but I knew there was a child coming into the world who needed a stable loving home. Did I question the choice that was made? Yes! A lot!

Ari had a lot of growing up to do, and now she had another human depending on her completely for his survival. Yes, we found out it was a boy, but there was no big gender reveal party celebration, as this had become such a stressful situation. As a family, we tried our best to be excited and joyous about a baby coming, but deep down I believe we all had concerns about this decision. Watching Ari struggle with the breakup and pregnancy was beyond difficult.

I began questioning my decisions and should I have let Ari make that final choice? Were Tyler's parents right? Do people think I forced Ari to keep this baby? Was this right or wrong? How will this work out?

Suddenly there was a huge blessing to enter our lives, the school-age parenting program at Central High School. Ari came home from school and explained how they had begun a program for all the students who were having babies. It was ironically my high school child development teacher who was running the program. Ari suddenly had a new click of friends. Months earlier watching her lose all her pom friends was so difficult and truly added to her emotions during pregnancy. At 16 to lose your boyfriend, father of your child, and all your friends, and plus watch your perfect little pom pon body growing a child in your belly, all this clearly played a huge part in her mental health. Ari struggled a lot mentally and emotionally and as her Mom it was so difficult to watch.

Soon Lisa Colla was taking over the school program and I knew instantly I loved this woman. Ari also loved her and the changes Lisa made in Ari's life were amazing. Suddenly Ari was with other young parents, learning how to deal with pregnancy and how to care for your growing body and baby and prepare for parenthood physically and emotionally. In addition, they learned how to navigate their final years in high school and keep goals of their own. Also how to navigate their final years in high school and keep goals of their own. The main objectives of shared journeys were to promote academic and parenting success allowing a bright future.

Ari's whole attitude about pregnancy and the situation with Tyler and her outlook on life changed. She was suddenly more positive and optimistic and I think really realizing she was going to be a MOM.

The final months of pregnancy our main focus was keeping Ari healthy, happy and distracted from Tyler and somewhat sane. It wasn't easy at times, but again I cannot stress what a blessing Lisa was in our lives. Lisa helped me as a mother navigate one of the most challenging times of my life. She also mentored and guided Ari through some real high school drama and issues. It was a horribly stressful and emotional time.

I remember throwing Ari a baby shower. Our family as a whole is a very strong loving family. We all did our best to embrace this pregnancy and a shower seemed like a good idea to keep Ari excited about the baby. It also was a party to welcome this baby we all knew we'd love and embrace. A portion of the guests were pom pon friends, sadly the few that remained friends with Ari. I remember thinking it was literally just a few years earlier I was hosting tea parties with Ari and her dolls and how did my life get to this.

The day Ari was admitted into the hospital in full labor was a day of huge emotions. Ari had wanted her sister Alex and I there with her in the delivery room. The labor went on all night and the three of us spent the night talking, laughing, and really bonding and preparing for the totally unknown. Seeing how Ari and Alex had really grown closer during this pregnancy was really a blessing. Watching your child, my youngest child, my baby, in labor was not easy. She was so young and watching her in such pain was heart-wrenching. Ari suddenly had a strength I never saw in her and I felt a renewed hope all was going to be okay.

Carter James was born June 29, 2011, at 10:56 am, weighing 7 lb 7 oz and 20 inches long. When the doctors placed Carter on Ari's chest, she bawled and said, "He's PERFECT!" I truly saw my baby finally as a Mother! The love she had for that tiny little boy in her arms validated any questions I had during the pregnancy. He was meant to be here! She was meant to be his mother!

When the time came to notify Tyler and his parents it was awkward, to say the least. When they said they wanted to come to the hospital we all felt such unease but without a doubt knew it was the right thing to do for Carter.

Heather brought Ari a gift of some lovely pajamas and again there was a lot of awkwardness. To say there was very little love between the families was an understatement.

Seeing Tyler and his parents meet Carter for the first time was such an eye-opener. The love they instantly felt for that boy was apparent. This was Carter's daddy and grandparents and he deserved all the love they had, despite the issues we had in the past months.

Ari came home from the hospital and quickly learned how challenging parenting was. My home now had a baby and that was not an easy adjustment for the family as a whole.

A few weeks after Carter was born Ari started suffering from horrible postpartum. I remember one evening Ari announcing to me she was putting him up for adoption. Again the flood of emotions and questioning my part in this kind of decision. Was this really happening? How could she even fathom such a thought. My heart literally hurt. This was my first grandson, the little boy who stole my heart the day he was born. How could she even say this?

Luckily this idea was brief and clearly only said out of postpartum depression. With medical help and time, Ari made it through the postpartum.

I knew from the day Carter entered the world he was Arianna's son and she had to take responsibility for this child. I began thinking it was too much for her and again questioning everything. Although it was tough Ari took complete responsibility. I watched my now 17-year-old daughter raise her son.

The next couple of months were challenging as Tyler and his parents wanted involvement.

When the decision was made during the pregnancy that Ari was having the baby and keeping him, we made clear they were not obligated and we would not ask anything of them. Suddenly to have them wanting to be so involved was sort of shocking and a bit scary. We questioned suddenly if they were going to fight for full custody. We truly wanted the best life for Carter, but we were very unsure how this would work between the families.

We literally took this all day by day.

Again the blessing Lisa Colla was in entering our life. She truly helped Ari and myself through some of the most difficult times. The program was such a blessing. Ari began teaching Carter sign language and before he could even speak he knew signs for "milk," "more," and "food." He was communicating before a year old.

At 8-month-old Carter would often grab a book of his and crawl into my lap to read. He loved being read books. It was amazing.

Ari was growing up fast and it made me so proud to watch. She was (and still is) an amazing mother. The love she has for Carter is undeniable.

It was a crazy first year for Carter and slowly we began to trust Tyler and his parents. They truly adored Carter.

It really became clear to us that Carter wasn't just Ari's son, he was Tyler's son also. Despite any bad moments during the pregnancy, Carter deserved the best and that included his Mom and Dad and their families. I watched Ari grow and mature and learn the true meaning of being a mother. Sometimes when her 17-year-old mind wanted to be spiteful and petty she learned it wasn't about her, it was about Carter.

Through some twist of fate soon after Carter was born I lost my full-time job. Kevin and I decided it best I stay home with Carter while Ari finishes high school and begins college. Kevin not only solely supported his family, but my daughter and her son—something I'm so grateful to him for. It was an amazing time to be home full-time with Carter and watch my daughter make plans for a career. That time I spent as a full-time grandmother was a time I will forever cherish.

The involvement of Tyler and his parents was also a huge blessing. It was established very early on there would be no set schedule, we would all work together for Carter's sake. When school and life were very hectic for Ari, Tyler and his parents would take Carter extra days. Ari and Tyler slowly grew into friends and always did what was best for Carter.

It was around that time Lisa told me the school-age parenting program was going to be a charter school and they needed a governing board. Lisa said they would like one of the parents of a student on the board and I was honored she asked me. I gladly said yes as there isn't much I wouldn't do for Lisa. (As I write this right now, I still feel such gratitude for her impact on Ari and Carter's life.)

The school was named Shared Journeys and it was truly a blessing to be involved. My involvement was very minimal but just seeing these young students all flourish as parents and young adults going on to college was amazing.

Ari always took full responsibility for Carter in my home and when he was still a small toddler Ari moved out with her new boyfriend.

Was it hard watching my baby and my first grandchild leave my home? Yes. But I can honestly say it was also a moment of such pride I felt for Ari as she was really growing up. I can honestly say she is hands down one of the best mothers I've ever known.

That boyfriend didn't last and Ari was faced with being a single mom living on her own. Not only did she survive, she thrived. Always keeping Carter and his younger brother first in her priorities. Ari began a whole new career in funeral services and that is where she met her now husband.

Tyler continued living at home and started his own schooling and career. With the help of Heather and Larry, they share custody with Ari. There is still really no set schedule as they work around Carter and everyone's schedule. Carter is always the main focus.

Always.

The families have not only remained civil but have grown into a very strong loving unit because of Carter.

To think of the bad feelings I had with Heather and Larry 13 years ago is hard to even imagine as I truly respect and adore them! They have been a huge amazing part of Carter's life. The influence they have on Carter is amazing. Tyler has grown to be a great dad. Carter truly idolizes his dad and their bond is awesome!

Carter just turned 12 this year. He is beyond a brilliant and charming young man. He is caring and kind and so well-rounded. I've never learned so much from a child as I have from him. His sense of humor is also one of a kind. We all agree he must be an old soul reincarnated.

Recently we had a baby shower for Ari who is now 29 years old, married and expecting her first daughter. Heather came to the shower, again bringing an amazing gift. She's always been an awesome gift giver. As soon as she arrived she went over and hugged my parents and my aunt. There have been many birthdays and baseball games shared with our two families and it just feels like one big extended family now. To see the love between everyone is so heartwarming.

We also recently celebrated Carter's 6th grade graduation together and going out for dinner and hanging out is not only far from awkward, but completely the norm and truly enjoyable.

This boy was not planned that is for sure, but he was welcomed and loved by so many. He has made his parents into amazing adults. He has brought two families very close.

The past 12 years have been miraculous.

They say it takes a village to raise a child and it's very true.

I could have never predicted how this village would have come together, but with open hearts and minds, and a lot of love, it has. ❤️

5

Joan's Story: My Thoughts from Support to Mentoring

After teaching and leading at-risk and students with learning differences for nearly 40 years. I was asked to help consult with Lisa Colla and a Governing Board team to develop and implement an Instrumentality Charter High School for pregnant and teen parents in the District of WAWM in West Allis, WI. Twelve years later, Shared Journeys Charter High School has

VH-studio/Shutterstock.com

grown from the vision/mission statements developed by the school's governing board stated: "academic and parenting success" to an honored and awarded charter high school for pregnant and teen parents. How was this accomplished? Central to the success was a focus on these areas while asking oneself important questions.

Focus on the Students and Their Babies/Children

a. What do teens need to become a successful parent? Build interactive and real-life curriculum including prenatal, birthing, child development, career planning, financial planning, relationship building, and alcohol and drug abuse prevention. Hold monthly "family nights including the children, network with community health, family, and business resources that can support students and their children.

b. What do pregnant and teen parents need to succeed academically? Teen parents need flexible curricula, school hours, and structures that support opportunities for success. All students should have an adult mentor.

c. What are the barriers to students' success? The biggest barrier to pregnant and teen parent success is getting to school each day. Why? Daycare problems. Most teen parents have difficulty securing childcare when attending school. If a caregiver is not available, often students are not in attendance. For that reason, pregnant and teen-parent charter schools need two things: (i) variable schedules with attendance waivers so that students are allowed to attend hybrid or offsite, and (ii) adjacent childcare rooms or options for childcare near the pregnant teen and parent classroom. Shared Journeys has had an Infant Lab available to students since the fall of 2018. It takes a lot of work to organize, find staff and an adequate facility, and gather equipment for a childcare center.

Focus on Great Teaching and Leadership

a. What kind of teacher leader is needed for a pregnant and teen parent charter? Organized, kind, great sense of humor, loves teenagers, and cares deeply about student success. A successful leader always finds ways to learn new skills, and curriculum, and isn't afraid to connect with community resources. If the leader doesn't know about something, they find someone who can step up and be a resource. Leaders of at-risk youth know they are "there" for all of the "kids" even after hours. They stay connected because students may or may not have someone to turn to.

b. Who supports the leadership, teachers, staff, and students? Everyone who has a genuine love of teen parents! Every charter needs the support of a team and a larger learning community. Although Shared Journeys was an instrumentality of a large metropolitan school district, it was supported by a charter governing board that developed a mission, vision, and bylaws and eventually incorporated as a 501C3. The Shared Journeys Governing Board oversaw the budget, and immediate needs of the school under the teacher/leader direction, and still reported out annually to the West Allis/West Milwaukee School District at large. Initially, the school obtained three Wisconsin State Charter Grants to develop, write and implement a charter school over three years. After the initial grants ended the teacher leader with the assistance of others, applied for and received a federal Inspire grant followed by a number of very generous grant rewards from area foundations and businesses. A charter school cannot function without grant assistance.

c. What other community support is needed for a teen parent Charter school? In addition to the governing board, it is most important for a teen parent charter to reach out and include many community groups in the mission. Shared Journeys has had many community connections including: Community educators in financial literacy, mentors for each student, a group of retired teachers (angels) that provides many necessities for the students in need, the local rotary and chamber club, the community foundation groups, area college and university interns and groups, Drug and alcohol prevention groups, local law enforcement education groups, the city health department educators, health organizations, and the many wonderful volunteers who come and hold babies in the infant lab. I was very fortunate to be a part of this process, become a mentor, and a governing board member, and watch so many wonderful teen parents (both young ladies and men) graduate from high school and continue their career and life journey as a loving parent and community member. The most rewarding aspect of being a part of Shared Journeys is becoming a mentor to a new mother 11 years ago. A strong mentoring program was developed that had many alumni educators and community members as mentors. When I became a mentor, I had no idea the powerful and loving relationship that would be made. Initially, my mentee struggled with the challenges of becoming a parent at 15 and learning to be a mother of a newborn infant. She was dealing with the physical changes after delivering her baby and breastfeeding all while dealing with issues of academic struggles and low self-esteem, and I needed to learn to be there for her. Wonderfully, we connected and because of the incredible Shared Journeys school environment, she completed all coursework to graduate with her class and attained a high B average all while building necessary life skills and self-confidence. As she built her skills, she applied for and got a job at the school district coffee bistro and while working there, she began to investigate a career in the culinary field. Upon graduation from high school, her son was now growing ready and healthy for school, and she was entering the local technical school, MATC in the Culinary Arts Program. Three years later she graduated from MATC and started her first experience at a downtown riverwalk restaurant. Several years later she got a new position with one of the best restaurant groups in the city. Today, I proudly state she is a 26-year-old woman with an 11-year-old child who just started the 5th grade. She works a full-time position as a pastry chef and lives with her family on her own. I am so glad that we have remained close, as we have both been able to share our tough times (she lost her Mom and I lost my brother) as well as celebrate the good times (sharing promotions, raises, children, grandchildren's achievements, and lunch dates). I am honored to have her in my life, not as my student, but as my friend, a precious gift.

6

Pam's Story: Financial Literacy

How do you teach money principles to kids that are either homeless, from homes on government assistance, or from households that have very little knowledge of how money works? That is where I started when approached by Lisa Colla to help teach a segment on money. What I decided to do is to not talk above or below with the students, they deserved better than that, just like the adults I work with daily. We all come into the arena of money knowledge and management with whatever style we are surrounded

with as we grow up. It all comes down to education. This is a realization that I have observed over 34 years working in the financial industry. This was very obvious in the 12 years that I had the honor to meet some amazing young and motivated people. Many of the students had major trust issues with adult figures. This presented the obvious solution, to be honest and transparent about myself and show my desire to give them knowledge. Once you give someone knowledge, no one can take it away. This resonated with them because many of the students had very little of their own. For them to know that they can have something that no one can take away made them feel like they had some power in their life. First, what to start with of course, the basics! The Rule of 72. This equation, developed by Albert Einstein, shows how money works and how the financial industry works and doesn't work. By sharing my story of learning this foundation piece (and how even having a college degree I never learned this), how I was a picture for doing everything wrong financially, how I learned to do better, and how it changed my life truly made an impact with the students. We all have stories of how we can make better choices with our money, but these students usually hadn't heard adults be honest about mistakes they had made. The main areas over this building block foundation of the Rule of 72 are: both good and bad debt, monthly budgeting, income necessary to support a family, basic banking, how to create good credit, insurance basics and investing. As you can already see, the concepts of money seemed to take the back seat to each student's personal financial literacy and upbringing. It was very important to keep the information relevant to how it could directly impact them for optimal learning to take place. I'm not naïve enough to believe that every student was listening with rapt attention. However, the goal became sharing enough so that they were in the know of resources available.

Before going into business, I was a police officer. Working with the public showed me how people didn't have fundamentals to move through life in many facets. With the students, it was important to connect the dots. Due to many of the students' circumstances, they qualified for numerous types of financial aid; rent assistance: childcare, food stamps, transportation, energy assistance, and education/tuition assistance. So having prior knowledge of these systems from my past background helped me to guide them, answer questions, and understand what they were dealing with. Describing to students the resources available was also important to show them how those areas of support could be a huge launching point for them to create a strong foundation financially. The goal was always to have them live "lean and mean" for the first five years.

By the end of 5 years, they would have positioned themselves to be able to move off assistance.

The giving of "a hand up versus a handout" was another underlying principle that I tried to interweave in our conversations. Lisa did a great job of integrating a giving back philosophy so that each would look at what they could be grateful for as well as what would each of them do to support others in the community. The conversations would many times take us down detailed discussions of some personal happenings in their own lives. For example, a student's mom had taken her social security number to open lines of credit and then max them out. Another student asked if it was normal to have two social security numbers, finding out later that a family member had been involved in fraud. Another parent of a student was claiming their grandchild on their tax forms even though the student was 18 and had filed taxes claiming their own child. Yet another student's parent wanted him to file for assistance so that this parent could utilize the services. Some students had parents that had filed bankruptcy multiple times, and they said they learned they could just buy whatever they wanted and then they could just file bankruptcy too. There were many stories that called for a lot of work to solve. Flexibility was key here and Lisa allowed for this to happen within the school day. It was important for this at-risk population to be heard. I always gave them a notebook to keep notes. To this day I see alumni who use this notebook as a reference and contact me with questions. Some are even clients of mine now.

The success of the alumni is very rewarding. One young man who would nod off in class apologized. I asked him if there was anything I could do to help him be more engaged. He said he worked third shift at night, went to school during the day and helped care for his child in the afternoon until work. Not only did he graduate with his high school diploma, but attended Milwaukee Area Technical College where he became a certified barber. He bought a home, and has now opened a barber shop.

It has been a joy to be part of this aspect of education and for this specific high-risk student population! Anyone wanting to put in place a charter school to service this population will do well to follow the template that Lisa has put together and is shared here in this book. I would go a bit further and encourage all school districts to incorporate a basic financial literacy class into their mandatory classes for students. Not stock clubs, but fundamentals, money touches everyone's lives wherever they go after high school. At the beginning of each semester, each student was a name, and by the end of the semester their individual stories gave them each a special place in my heart, and I hope they do in yours.

It takes a village!